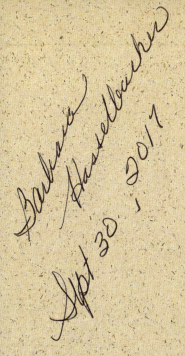
Barbara Hasselbacher
Sept 30, 2017

THE RECIPES OF THE

Five Brothers

VOLUME I

Five Brothers One Passion

THE RECIPES OF THE FIVE BROTHERS ~ VOLUME I

Book Design:	Bart Goodell
Photography:	Jeff Weir
Writer/Editor:	Leah Rosch
Recipe Development:	Rosemary Smalberg
Food Styling:	Michael DiBeneditto
Prop Styling:	Sylvia Lachter
Hand Lettering:	Bernard Maisner
Creative Direction:	Jeff Brall
Digital Production:	Rich Graham

Many thanks to all of these individuals who helped in making this
book a reality; Steve Luttmann, Julie Ying, Ginnie Blake-West, Larry Kadish,
Bonnie Guest, Gail Young, Hank Gelinas, Renée Tannenbaum and Jerry Simpson.

ISBN 0-9655889-0-4

Printed in Hong Kong

L'amore per la buona tavola
é amore per la vita

A passion for food is a passion for life

Contenuto

INTRODUCTION

ONE OF THE HALLMARKS OF LIFE IN THE TUSCAN COUNTRYSIDE IS HEARTY FARE THAT WARMS THE SOUL AS WELL AS THE body. Robust, honest, and flavorful, the food from the land of the Five Brothers has the power to bring friends and family closer together and to banish the tensions of the working day. Stews, roasts, piping-hot pasta dishes and soups you can practically eat with a fork are mainstays of the Tuscan kitchen. It is food that expresses beautifully the Five Brothers passion for eating well and living well, the same passion that inspired the exquisite sauces that bear the Five Brothers name and that you'll find at the heart of many of the recipes that follow.

The four menus that appear herein differ considerably from one another. But they all share the Tuscan passion for quality ingredients elegantly prepared and shared in good company. While each of these menus has been assembled with care to provide a balance of flavors, textures and colors, you're sure to find that the full-bodied main dishes at the heart of these meals, such as the LASAGNA ALLA FIORENTINA or the RISOTTO CON PANCETTA, are sufficient to satisfy hungry friends and family members on their own. And the appetizers and salads you'll find here, such as the CROSTINI CON RICOTTA ALLE VERDURE or the ANTIPASTO MISTO, will evoke warm smiles whether they're served by themselves as an afternoon snack or as part of a multi-course dinner served to a large gathering. And when it's time to really celebrate with good cheer, good friends and a gala meal, the festive brunch at the end will fit the bill with ease; this is one menu that should be savored from soup to nuts (or in this case, from crostini to biscotti).

So whether you're entertaining a large gathering of friends or preparing a quick meal for the family, indulge yourself and your loved ones with these soothing and delectable samplings of CUCINA TOSCANA—the original comfort food. 🍂

Cena casalinga toscana

TUSCAN KITCHEN SUPPER

This selection works equally well as a restorative dinner for the family or as a casual Saturday night supper for close friends. The sumptuous Ribollita, Tuscany's famous bread soup, is practically a meal in itself. For your second course, this rich spinach lasagna will be most appreciated; or opt for the orecchiette when catering to lighter appetites. And this effortless dessert offers a light, sweetly satisfying finale. Serves four to six.

RIBOLLITA
tuscan bread soup

LASAGNA ALLA FIORENTINA
spinach alfredo lasagna

— or —

ORECCHIETTE CON SPINACI E FAGIOLI CANNELLINI
orecchiette with greens and beans

SCAROLA TIEPIDA CON UVETTA E PINOLI
wilted escarole with raisins and pine nuts

PERE COTTE
poached pears

ribollita

Ribollita

Tuscan Bread Soup

*The secret to this hearty and satisfying soup: Allow mixture to stand
and thicken long enough that it begs to be eaten with a fork.*

1 LOAF STALE CRUSTY TUSCAN BREAD,
  CUT INTO CUBES (ABOUT 8 CUPS)
4 CUPS COLD WATER
2/3 CUP OLIVE OIL
3 CLOVES GARLIC, MINCED
2 TABLESPOONS CHOPPED FRESH SAGE
1/2 CUP CHOPPED CELERY
1 LARGE ONION, CHOPPED

1 JAR (26 OZ.) FIVE BROTHERS™
  SPICY PEPPER TRIO SAUCE
5 CUPS CHICKEN OR BEEF BROTH,
  HEATED
SALT AND PEPPER TO TASTE
OLIVE OIL TO TASTE
FRESH SAGE FOR GARNISH

Place bread in a large bowl; sprinkle with water until bread is evenly moistened. Let bread soak about 10 minutes. Squeeze bread as dry as possible; separate into pieces and set aside.

In a large saucepan, heat olive oil; add garlic and sage; sauté lightly about 3 to 4 minutes. Add celery and onion; cook until vegetables are tender. Add bread; stir to evenly coat bread with oil. Add sauce to bread mixture. Stir in hot broth, season with salt and pepper. Bring to a boil; cover and remove from heat. Let stand for 1 hour. Stir mixture to break up remaining bread cubes. Reheat over low heat. Serve in rimmed bowls; drizzle with olive oil before serving, if desired. Garnish with fresh sage leaves.

Serves 6.

This recipe is a lighter variation on the classic country-style soup. For greater authenticity, add 1 cup cooked and drained cannellini beans and 1 pound Savoy cabbage, cut into 1/2-inch strips, before bringing soup to a boil.

Lasagne alla fiorentina

SPINACH ALFREDO LASAGNA

*Spinach elevates this crowd-pleasing standard to
special status. Alfredo sauce gives it a rich, new twist.*

1 PACKAGE (10 OZ.) FROZEN CHOPPED
SPINACH, THAWED AND SQUEEZED
DRY

2 POUNDS PART-SKIM RICOTTA CHEESE

8 OUNCES SHREDDED PART-SKIM
MOZZARELLA CHEESE

½ CUP GRATED PARMESAN CHEESE,
DIVIDED

2 EGGS

SALT AND PEPPER TO TASTE

1 JAR (26 OZ.) FIVE BROTHERS™
FRESH TOMATO BASIL SAUCE

1 PACKAGE (16 OZ.) LASAGNA
NOODLES, COOKED AND DRAINED

1 JAR (17 OZ.) FIVE BROTHERS™
CREAMY ALFREDO SAUCE

Preheat oven to 375° F.

In a large bowl, thoroughly combine spinach, ricotta and mozzarella cheeses, ¼ cup Parmesan cheese, eggs, salt and pepper. Pour ¾ cup Fresh Tomato Basil sauce evenly in a 13 x 9-inch baking dish. Layer 4 lasagna noodles over sauce. Spread half the spinach-cheese mixture over noodles. Top with 1 cup Fresh Tomato Basil sauce. Repeat layers ending with lasagna noodles. Evenly spread Creamy Alfredo sauce over the top of the lasagna. Sprinkle with ¼ cup Parmesan cheese. Cover and bake 1 hour. Uncover, bake 10 minutes or until bubbly. Allow lasagna to sit 10 minutes before serving.

Serves 6-8.

For traditional ground-beef lasagna, omit spinach and replace with 1 pound cooked, drained ground beef. Combine with Fresh Tomato Basil sauce and layer in lasagna along with cheese filling and noodles.

orecchiette with greens and beans

Orecchiette con spinaci e fagioli cannellini

ORECCHIETTE WITH GREENS AND BEANS

These pasta shapes are the perfect receptacles for this dish's riches.
Bacon provides a smoky essence; spinach mellows when cooked.

1 JAR (26 OZ.) FIVE BROTHERS™
   FRESH TOMATO BASIL SAUCE
1 PACKAGE (10 OZ.) FRESH SPINACH
4 SLICES BACON, CHOPPED
3 CLOVES GARLIC, MINCED
1 SMALL ONION, CHOPPED

1 CAN (16 OZ.) WHITE BEANS,
   DRAINED AND RINSED
1 PACKAGE (16 OZ.) ORECCHIETTE OR
   SHELL PASTA, COOKED AND DRAINED

In a medium saucepan, heat sauce thoroughly; set aside. Thoroughly wash spinach in cold water; remove and discard stems. Tear spinach leaves coarsely; set aside. In a large skillet, cook bacon until crisp; drain fat. In the same skillet, sauté garlic and onion until tender. Add beans; cook over low heat until heated through, stirring occasionally.

Add spinach to skillet; cover and cook just until spinach is wilted. Spoon heated sauce over hot pasta. Top with bean and spinach mixture; toss to coat well.

Serves 6.

Scarola tiepida con uvetta e pinoli

WILTED ESCAROLE WITH RAISINS AND PINE NUTS

The pairing of sweet raisins and pine nuts softens the bite of the dressing in this unusually pretty salad.

2 POUNDS FRESH ESCAROLE, TRIMMED

2 TABLESPOONS OLIVE OIL

1 CLOVE GARLIC, MINCED

2 TABLESPOONS GOLDEN RAISINS

2 TABLESPOONS TOASTED PINE NUTS

2 TEASPOONS RED WINE VINEGAR

SALT AND PEPPER TO TASTE

Thoroughly wash escarole in cold water; tear leaves coarsely. Steam escarole just until wilted, about 1 to 2 minutes. Remove and set aside. In a large skillet, sauté garlic in olive oil. Add escarole, raisins, pine nuts, vinegar, salt and pepper; stir to mix well. Warm lightly. Serve on individual salad plates.

Serves 6.

Pinoli Most famous for their flavorful addition to classic pesto sauce, Italian pine nuts, or PINOLI, perk up a variety of sweet and savory dishes as well. They come from the large cones of the stone pine tree native to Italy. The process to extract these meaty little nuts is quite labor-intensive, which explains why they're so prohibitively priced. But their delicate, nutty flavor is worth the cost (and any recipe that suggests substituting slivered almonds is not to be trusted). Pine nuts turn rancid very quickly due to their high fat content, but they can be stored safely in an airtight container in the freezer for up to nine months or in the refrigerator for up to three.

wilted escarole with raisins and pine nuts

poached pears

Pere cotte

POACHED PEARS

*For a pretty and fool-proof presentation, pick pears that
are not overly ripe and have gracefully shaped stems.*

6 BOSC PEARS	5 WHOLE CLOVES
2 CUPS WATER	ZEST OF 1 LEMON, CUT IN
1 CUP SUGAR	STRIPS
2 CINNAMON STICKS	JUICE OF ½ LEMON

Peel pears, leaving stem intact. Using a small melon baller, remove stems and seeds
from bottom of pears. In a saucepan that will accommodate pears upright, combine
water, sugar, cinnamon sticks, cloves, lemon zest and lemon juice. Bring to a boil. Add
pears, cook over medium heat, maintaining a boil for 5 minutes. Remove from heat,
allow pears to cool slowly. Baste pears occasionally with poaching liquid. When
completely cooled, chill pears. Serve on individual dessert plates; spoon liquid over
pears.

Serves 6.

Cenetta davanti al caminetto

FIRESIDE DINNER PARTY

*S*erve this quintessential hearty fare when temperatures are low
and watch your guests light (and warm) up. Call the party for an early start,
as this is one meal that should not be rushed. While preparation may
entail the better part of an afternoon, none of these recipes require
last-minute tending. That means when the doorbell rings, everything
will be ready and waiting. Serves six.

FOCACCIA ALLE VONGOLE E PANCETTA
clam and bacon focaccia

CREMA DI GAMBERI
shrimp bisque

FILETTO DI MANZO ARROSTO ALLE ERBE
herb roasted beef tenderloin

INSALATA TOSCANA DI PANE E FAGIOLI
tuscan bean and bread salad

CROSTATA DI NOCI E MIRTILLI ROSSI
cranberry walnut tart

shrimp bisque

Focaccia alle vongole e pancetta

CLAM AND BACON FOCACCIA

*This flavorful variation on basic focaccia (a versatile Italian flat bread)
can be savored served warm or at room temperature.*

½ RECIPE BAKED FOCACCIA BREAD
½ CUP FIVE BROTHERS™ ALFREDO
SAUCE WITH MUSHROOMS
¼ CUP TORN FRESH BASIL LEAVES
4 OUNCES FRESH MOZZARELLA
CHEESE, DRAINED AND SLICED

1 CAN (6½ OZ.) MINCED CLAMS,
DRAINED
3 STRIPS BACON, COOKED AND
CRUMBLED

Preheat oven to 425°F.

Prepare and bake focaccia as directed below. Spoon Alfredo Sauce with Mushrooms sauce over focaccia. Top with basil leaves, mozzarella slices, minced clams and crumbled bacon. Bake 8 to 10 minutes. Serves 6.

Focaccia

5 CUPS UNBLEACHED
ALL-PURPOSE FLOUR
2 TSP. SALT
2 CUPS WARM WATER
(105°-115° F.)
1 PKG. (¼ OZ.) DRY YEAST
3 TBSP. EXTRA-VIRGIN
OLIVE OIL PLUS
ADDITIONAL OLIVE OIL
FOR DRIZZLING

In a large bowl, combine flour and salt; set aside. In another bowl, combine warm water with yeast; stir until yeast dissolves. Whisk in olive oil. Add yeast mixture to flour. Mix on low speed using an electric mixer about 2 minutes or until well combined. Remove dough from bowl; knead until a smooth ball of dough forms. Place dough in bowl; cover and let rise 60 to 90 minutes or until doubled. Generously oil a 17 x 13-inch baking sheet with additional olive oil. Place dough in pan; press and stretch dough evenly with oiled fingers to fill pan. Pierce the dough with a fork at 1-inch intervals. Drizzle lightly with olive oil. Cover the focaccia dough and let rise about 45 minutes or until doubled. Preheat oven to 450° F. Bake focaccia about 20 minutes or until golden brown. Place on a rack to cool. Serve as a bread or use as a base for focaccia toppings.

Crema di gamberi

SHRIMP BISQUE

*Simmering the shrimp in the soup intensifies the flavor of
this rich, zesty and wonderfully welcoming first course.*

1   MEDIUM ONION, FINELY CHOPPED
1   STALK CELERY, FINELY CHOPPED
1   RED BELL PEPPER, CHOPPED
2   CLOVES GARLIC, MINCED
2   TABLESPOONS BUTTER
1   JAR (26 OZ.) FIVE BROTHERS[TM]
    FRESH TOMATO BASIL SAUCE

1   JAR (17 OZ.) FIVE BROTHERS[TM]
    CREAMY ALFREDO SAUCE
1   CAN (13¾ OZ.) LOWER SALT
    CHICKEN BROTH
    TABASCO SAUCE, TO TASTE
12 OUNCES FRESH OR FROZEN SHRIMP,
    PEELED AND DEVEINED
    PARSLEY FOR GARNISH

In a large saucepan, sauté onion, celery, red pepper and garlic in butter until tender. Add Fresh Tomato Basil and Creamy Alfredo sauces; stir to mix well. Add chicken broth and Tabasco sauce; simmer over low heat about 15 minutes, stirring occasionally. Add shrimp; cook until shrimp just turns pink. Serve bisque garnished with parsley.

Serves 6.

herb roasted beef tenderloin

Filetto di manzo arrosto alle erbe

HERB ROASTED BEEF TENDERLOIN

*Garlic cloves are the secret tenderizer, baby vegetables the
picturesque accompaniment, in this savory one-pot dish.*

1 WHOLE BEEF TENDERLOIN
(ABOUT 5 LBS.) TRIMMED
1 TABLESPOON OLIVE OIL
1 TEASPOON SALT
1 TEASPOON GROUND BLACK PEPPER
3 CLOVES GARLIC, FINELY CHOPPED
ROSEMARY SPRIGS FOR GARNISH
1 TABLESPOON FINELY CHOPPED FRESH
FLAT-LEAF ITALIAN PARSLEY

PORTOBELLO MUSHROOM SAUCE:
2 PACKAGES (6 OZ. EACH) SLICED
PORTOBELLO MUSHROOMS
3 TABLESPOONS UNSALTED BUTTER
½ CUP DRY RED WINE OR BEEF BROTH
½ CUP FIVE BROTHERS™ OVEN-
ROASTED GARLIC & ONION SAUCE
½ CUP HEAVY CREAM

Rub beef tenderloin with olive oil. Season with salt, pepper, garlic and parsley. Wrap roast with plastic wrap and marinate in refrigerator at least 4 hours overnight.

Preheat oven to 425°. Place meat in shallow baking pan. Roast 45 minutes or until meat thermometer reaches 130° for rare. Let stand 5 minutes before carving. Meanwhile, prepare Portobello Mushroom Sauce. Serve with sauce.

PORTOBELLO MUSHROOM SAUCE: In skillet, cook 2 packages (6 oz. each) sliced portobello mushrooms in 3 tablespoons unsalted butter; set aside. Add ½ cup dry red wine or beef broth and ½ cup Oven-Roasted Garlic and Onion Sauce; heat gently. Remove from heat and stir in ½ cup heavy cream.

Serves 8.

Insalata toscana di pane e fagioli

TUSCAN BEAN AND BREAD SALAD

*This salad/side dish deliciously displays the wonders Tuscans work with
days-old bread. Make more than you need—it's even better the next day.*

1 LOAF CRUSTY STALE BREAD, TORN IN
  BITE-SIZE PIECES
  APPROXIMATELY ½ CUP WATER
1 SMALL ONION, CHOPPED
2 CLOVES GARLIC, MINCED
2 STALKS CELERY, THINLY SLICED
¼ CUP OIL-CURED OLIVES, PITTED
1 CAN (15½ OZ.) WHITE BEANS,
  DRAINED AND RINSED

½ CUP FIVE BROTHERS™ FRESH
  TOMATO BASIL SAUCE
2 TABLESPOONS OLIVE OIL
2 TABLESPOONS BALSAMIC VINEGAR
2 TABLESPOONS MINCED PARSLEY
1 TEASPOON MINCED FRESH SAGE
1 TEASPOON FINELY GRATED ORANGE
  ZEST
  SALT AND PEPPER TO TASTE

Sprinkle just enough water over bread to moisten without making it soggy; set aside. In a medium bowl, combine remaining ingredients; stir to mix well. Serve salad over moistened bread.

Serves 6.

tuscan bean and bread salad

cranberry walnut tart

Crostata di noci e mirtilli rossi

CRANBERRY WALNUT TART

Sweet-tart cranberries give this delicacy a distinctly sophisticated appeal.
If fresh berries aren't available, frozen will work just as beautifully.

DOUGH:
- 1 CUP FLOUR
- 2 TABLESPOONS SUGAR
- ¼ TEASPOON SALT

- 4 TABLESPOONS COLD UNSALTED BUTTER, CUT IN CUBES
- ½ TEASPOON FINELY GRATED LEMON RIND
- 2½ TABLESPOONS ICE WATER

In a food processor, combine flour, sugar and salt. Pulse briefly to combine. Add chilled butter and lemon rind, pulse 10 to 12 times or until butter mixture resembles coarse oatmeal. With food processor running, add ice water all at once. Process for about 10 seconds until a ball of dough forms. Turn dough onto a sheet of plastic wrap. Flatten to form a 7-inch circle. Wrap dough tightly and refrigerate at least 1 hour.

FILLING:
- 2 CUPS CRANBERRIES
- ½ CUP CHOPPED WALNUTS

- 3 TABLESPOONS SUGAR
- 2 TABLESPOONS BROWN SUGAR
- CONFECTIONERS SUGAR

Roll dough into an 11-inch circle on a lightly floured surface. Place dough on a baking sheet. In a large bowl, thoroughly combine cranberries, walnuts, sugar and brown sugar. Spoon cranberry mixture over crust leaving about a 1-inch border around the outside edge. Fold dough over cranberries, pinching as necessary to keep it in place. Bake 15 to 18 minutes, or until crust is golden and berries are juicy. Cool on a rack about 10 minutes. Dust with sifted confectioner's sugar. Serve warm.

Serves 6-8.

Pranzo del sabato fra amici

COZY SATURDAY LUNCH

*H*ere's a great lunch for a day of outdoor activity. Be sure to prepare plenty
of the crostini—these delightful toasts with their creamy topping are sure to be gobbled
up by grown-ups and kids alike. The soothingly spicy bean soup and the robust risotto serve
equally well as satisfying main courses. The warm radicchio dish is a tasty alternative
to plain old salad. And these cookies make a lovely last course. Serves four to six.

CROSTINI CON RICOTTA ALLE VERDURE
garden crostini

ZUPPA DI FAGIOLI PICCANTE
hot bean soup

— *or* —

RISOTTO CON PANCETTA
risotto with pancetta

RADICCHIO E CAVOLO CON SALSA D'ACCIUGHE ALLE ERBE
radicchio and cabbage with herbed anchovy sauce

AMARETTI FINI
almond macaroon crisps

hot bean soup

Crostini con ricotta alle verdure

GARDEN CROSTINI

*Here's an easy antipasto, hors d'oeuvre—or anytime snack. Be decadent and
prepare with whole-milk ricotta; anything less just won't be as luscious.*

8 OUNCES RICOTTA

3 TABLESPOONS FINELY CHOPPED
   FRESH BASIL

2 TABLESPOONS FINELY CHOPPED
   SCALLIONS

1 TABLESPOON FINELY CHOPPED
   FRESH PARSLEY

1 TABLESPOON OLIVE OIL

1 SMALL CARROT, PEELED AND FINELY
   SHREDDED
   SALT AND PEPPER TO TASTE

3 TABLESPOONS UNSALTED BUTTER,
   SOFTENED

12 THIN BAGUETTE SLICES

Preheat oven to 400° F.

In a medium bowl, thoroughly combine ricotta, basil, scallions, parsley, olive oil, carrot, salt
and pepper. Stir until well blended. Lightly butter bread slices and place on a baking sheet
buttered-side up. Bake about 8 minutes until crisp and lightly browned. Spoon ricotta mixture
over crostini. Best served warm.

Makes 12 crostini.

Zuppa di fagioli piccante

HOT BEAN SOUP

*The combination of cauliflower and Tuscan cuisine's favorite
beans adds great texture to this piquant main-course soup.*

1 CLOVE GARLIC, MINCED
1/8 TEASPOON CRUSHED RED
PEPPER FLAKES
1 TABLESPOON OLIVE OIL
2 CANS (16 OZ. EACH) CANNELLINI
BEANS, DRAINED AND RINSED
2 CUPS COOKED FRESH
CAULIFLOWER FLORETS

1 JAR (17 OZ.) FIVE BROTHERS™
CREAMY ALFREDO SAUCE
2 CUPS CHICKEN STOCK
2 TABLESPOONS CHOPPED PARSLEY
2 TABLESPOONS CHOPPED BASIL
GRATED PARMESAN CHEESE
TUSCAN HERB BREAD

In a saucepan, lightly sauté garlic and crushed red pepper flakes in olive oil. Remove from heat.
Coarsely purée beans and cauliflower in a food processor or blender. Add bean and cauliflower
purée, Creamy Alfredo sauce and chicken stock to garlic. Cook over low heat, stirring occasionally
until heated through. Add fresh parsley and basil just before serving. Serve with Parmesan cheese
and Tuscan herb bread.

Serves 4-6.

risotto with pancetta

Risotto con pancetta

RISOTTO WITH PANCETTA

*Though it may seem painstaking, continuous stirring is the true trick to achieving
the creamiest consistency in this special risotto dish.*

6 OUNCES PANCETTA OR BACON,
  CHOPPED

3 TABLESPOONS OLIVE OIL

1 MEDIUM RED ONION, FINELY
  CHOPPED

1½ CUPS ARBORIO RICE

2 TEASPOON FINELY CHOPPED
  FRESH ROSEMARY OR ¼ TEASPOON
  DRIED ROSEMARY

2 CUPS DRY RED WINE

½ JAR (26 OZ.) FIVE BROTHERS ^{TM}
  GRILLED SUMMER VEGETABLE
  SAUCE

5 CUPS CHICKEN BROTH

½ CUP GRATED PARMESAN CHEESE

In 8-inch skillet, lightly brown pancetta; drain and set aside. In large saucepan, heat oil and cook onion until tender. Stir in rice and rosemary; cook 1 minute. Add wine and cook until totally absorbed, stirring frequently.

Meanwhile, heat Grilled Summer Vegetable sauce and chicken broth. Add about 1½ cups heated sauce mixture to rice. Continue to cook over medium-low heat, stirring frequently (rice and liquid should maintain a low simmer.) Continue adding heated sauce mixture gradually. Cook, stirring constantly, 25 minutes or until rice is tender (rice should be moist and creamy). Stir in cheese and pancetta. Serve, if desired, with Tuscan bread and garnish with fresh sage leaves.

Serves 4-6.

Radicchio e cavolo con salsa d'acciughe alle erbe

RADICCHIO AND CABBAGE WITH
HERBED ANCHOVY SAUCE

For the most flavorful foundation, warm vegetables until the leaves are just wilted.

1 TEASPOON ANCHOVY PASTE
1 TABLESPOON DIJON MUSTARD
1 TABLESPOON LEMON JUICE
1 CLOVE GARLIC, CRUSHED
1/2 TEASPOON CHOPPED
  DRIED ROSEMARY
1 TABLESPOON MINCED PARSLEY

1/2 CUP OLIVE OIL, DIVIDED
1 SMALL HEAD RADICCHIO,
  QUARTERED LENGTHWISE
1 SMALL HEAD RED CABBAGE, SLICED
  IN WEDGES
  SALT AND PEPPER TO TASTE

In a small bowl, thoroughly combine anchovy paste, mustard, lemon juice, garlic, rosemary and parsley. Add 6 tablespoons olive oil while whisking to make a smooth sauce. Discard garlic.

Heat a large skillet over medium-high heat. Brush radicchio and red cabbage with remaining olive oil. Cook in preheated skillet 8 to 10 minutes, turning occasionally until tender. Season with salt and pepper. Stir sauce and serve over warm radicchio and cabbage. Serves 4-6.

Radicchio This trendy "lettuce" is actually burgundy-leafed Italian chicory. The most widely available varieties stateside are RADICCHIO DI VERONA and DI TREVISO. Both grow in small, tight heads and have firm, tender leaves with a slightly bitter taste. Choose heads with crisp, full-hued leaves that show no signs of browning. To prepare, discard the few outer leaves and tear—rather than cut or chop—the interior leaves for eating raw in salads; use whole leaves when sautéing, braising, baking or grilling. Fairly hearty, fresh radicchio can keep in the refrigerator for up to a week. For maximum shelf life, refrigerate unwashed in a tightly wrapped plastic bag.

radicchio and cabbage with herbed anchovy sauce, garden crostini

almond macaroon crisps

Amaretti fini

ALMOND MACAROON CRISPS

*These light confections will have you parting with store-bought amaretti
cookies for good. For tasteful authenticity, serve with espresso.*

¾ CUP BLANCHED ALMONDS,
VERY FINELY GROUND

¾ CUP SUGAR

2 LARGE EGG WHITES,
AT ROOM TEMPERATURE

¼ TEASPOON ALMOND EXTRACT

Preheat oven to 350° F.

Line 3 baking sheets with parchment paper or aluminum foil; set aside. In a large bowl, combine almonds and sugar; stir to mix well. In another bowl, whisk together egg whites and almond extract until soft peaks form. Add egg whites to the almond mixture. Stir to form a soft batter. With a teaspoon, spoon batter onto baking sheets, spacing cookies apart, about 12 cookies per sheet. Bake in the center of oven about 15 minutes or until lightly browned. Remove from oven and transfer parchment sheets to cooling racks until cookies begin to firm up, about 3 to 4 minutes. With a sharp knife, lift cookies from parchment and transfer to racks to cool completely.

Makes about 36 cookies.

Colazione festosa

FESTIVE BRUNCH BUFFET

*T*urn any day into a holiday with this simply spectacular brunch menu. It's as
impressive as it is easy to prepare. If you've never tasted roasted garlic,
you're in for a rare treat. The antipasto salad is certain to receive rave
reviews. This gnocchi dish raises pasta to celebratory status. And you may
want to make extra batches of these biscotti—they are, in a
word, fabulous. Serves eight to ten.

CROSTINI ALL'AGLIO ARROSTO
crostini with roasted garlic

ANTIPASTO MISTO
classic antipasto salad

GNOCCHI ALLA CREMA DI PEPERONI ROSSI
gnocchi with creamy roasted red pepper sauce

INSALATA TIEPIDA DI LENTICCHIE
warm lentil salad

BISCOTTI DI MANDORLE ALL'ANICE
almond anise biscotti

gnocchi with creamy roasted red pepper sauce
see page 38

roasted garlic

Crostini all'aglio arrosto

CROSTINI WITH ROASTED GARLIC

*The simple trick to roasting garlic is to use the whitest heads
you can find. Once roasted, the garlic spreads like butter.*

6 WHOLE GARLIC HEADS
   OLIVE OIL
2 CRUSTY BAGUETTES, SLICED
   ½-INCH THICK

6 TABLESPOONS UNSALTED BUTTER,
   SOFTENED
1 CUP FIVE BROTHERS™ MARINARA
   WITH BURGUNDY WINE SAUCE,
   HEATED

Preheat oven to 375° F.

Cut off papery tips of stem end of garlic heads. Brush liberally with olive oil. Place in a garlic roaster or wrap garlic heads tightly in foil and place in a shallow baking dish. Bake about 1 hour or until garlic is very soft, but not browned.

Lightly butter bread slices and place on a baking sheet buttered-side up. Bake 8 to 10 minutes until crisp and lightly browned. Spread toasted crostini with roasted garlic. Serve sauce as a dip, if desired.

Serves 10.

Antipasto misto

Classic Antipasto Salad

If time allows, prepare this salad days in advance; the flavors harmonize better the longer they're left to mingle.

⅓ CUP BOTTLED ITALIAN SALAD
   DRESSING

2 TABLESPOONS FIVE BROTHERS™
   MARINARA WITH BURGUNDY WINE
   SAUCE

2 LARGE CARROTS, SLICED

1 SMALL FENNEL BULB, CORED AND
   THINLY SLICED (OPTIONAL)

1 JAR (10 OZ.) PEPPERONCINI,
   DRAINED

1 JAR (6 OZ. EACH) ROASTED RED
   PEPPER STRIPS, OIL-CURED OLIVES
   AND MARINATED ARTICHOKE
   HEARTS, DRAINED

6 OUNCES MARINATED OR PLAIN
   BOCCONCINI (FRESH MOZZARELLA)

4 OUNCES PEPPERONI, SLICED

2 OUNCES DRAINED SUN-DRIED
   TOMATOES PACKED IN OIL, CUT INTO
   STRIPS

Combine bottled dressing and Marinara with Burgundy Wine Sauce; set aside.

In medium saucepan, cover carrots and fennel with water. Bring to a boil and cook 3 to 4 minutes or until crisp tender; drain and cool. In large bowl, combine all salad ingredients. Pour dressing over salad; toss. Cover and chill 4 hours or overnight. To serve, arrange on a platter and garnish, if desired, with fresh parsley and thyme.

Serves 8-10.

classic antipasto salad

Gnocchi alla crema di peperoni rossi

GNOCCHI WITH CREAMY ROASTED RED PEPPER SAUCE

*The roasted pepper purée is the Tuscan trade secret in this special pasta
course. If time allows, make the gnocchi from scratch.*

1 JAR (7 OZ.) ROASTED RED
PEPPERS, DRAINED
1 JAR (17 OZ.) FIVE BROTHERS^{TM}
CREAMY ALFREDO SAUCE
¼ CUP SHERRY WINE
3 DROPS TABASCO SAUCE

3 TABLESPOONS FINELY CHOPPED
FRESH BASIL
2 POUNDS FRESH OR FROZEN
GNOCCHI, COOKED AND DRAINED
BASIL LEAVES FOR GARNISH

Purée roasted peppers in a food processor or blender; set aside. In a medium saucepan, combine pepper purée, Alfredo sauce, sherry wine and Tabasco sauce; simmer over low heat about 10 minutes or until heated through. Remove from heat; stir in fresh basil. Spoon over hot gnocchi; toss to coat well. Garnish with basil leaves.

Serves 8.

HOMEMADE GNOCCHI IN FIVE STEPS

Italian for "dumplings," gnocchi aren't all that difficult to make—and homemade are so much tastier than the store-bought varieties. Classic gnocchi are made from potatoes, but they can also be made from flour or cornmeal. To make a six-person serving of gnocchi di patate, or potato gnocchi, you need:

2 POUNDS BAKING POTATOES,   ½ TEASPOON SALT
WASHED BUT NOT PEELED   2 CUPS FLOUR
1 EGG

1:   Steam potatoes until tender (about 30 minutes). While still hot, peel potatoes, place in a bowl and mash.

2:   Mix in the egg and salt, and turn mixture onto a floured board.

3:   Put a pot of salted water (about 6 quarts) to boil. Knead the dough for roughly 10 minutes, adding flour as necessary, until the mixture forms a firm, smooth dough.

4:   To form the dumplings, flour palms and board again. Break off small pieces of dough, and roll each into thin, cigar shapes with your palms. With a paring knife, cut each cylinder into inch-long pieces. Then gently press each piece on the tines of a fork—for those characteristic ridges—pressing each in the center with your thumb. Set shaped gnocchi on floured napkins; this helps to absorb the moisture from the potatoes.

5:   Drop the gnocchi, several at a time, into boiling water and cook for about three minutes, or until they rise to the surface. Remove cooked gnocchi with a slotted spoon, drain well; place on a platter and cover to keep warm while cooking remaining dumplings.

warm lentil salad

Insalata tiepida di lenticchie

Warm Lentil Salad

*In Tuscany, lentils are among the most popular staples. One taste
of this simple side dish and you'll instantly understand why.*

1 POUND DRY LENTILS
1 BAY LEAF
2 TEASPOONS FRESH THYME
6 CUPS CHICKEN BROTH, HOMEMADE
  OR CANNED
3 MEDIUM CARROTS, PEELED AND
  CHOPPED
1 WHOLE MEDIUM ONION, PEELED

$\frac{1}{2}$ CUP FRESH LEMON JUICE
$\frac{1}{2}$ CUP CHOPPED FRESH PARSLEY
$\frac{1}{4}$ CUP OLIVE OIL
$\frac{1}{4}$ CUP SLICED SCALLIONS
  SALT AND PEPPER TO TASTE
1 HEAD RADICCHIO, SEPARATED INTO
  LEAVES

In a large saucepan, combine lentils, bay leaf, thyme, carrots, onion and chicken broth; heat to boiling. Reduce heat to low; cover and simmer 20 to 25 minutes, until lentils are tender and broth is absorbed. Do not overcook. Remove and discard onion and bay leaf.

In a large bowl, combine lemon juice, parsley, olive oil and scallions. Add lentils and toss. Season with salt and pepper. Line individual bowls with radicchio leaves and top with lentil salad. Serve warm or at room temperature.

Serves 8-10.

Biscotti di mandorle all'anice

ALMOND ANISE BISCOTTI

*The tastiest way to eat these crunchy confections: Dip twice in
a glass of sweet Vin Santo, Tuscany's favorite dessert wine.*

2½ CUPS FLOUR

2 TEASPOONS ANISE SEEDS

1½ TEASPOONS BAKING POWDER

½ TEASPOON SALT

½ CUP BUTTER, SOFTENED

1 CUP SUGAR

1 TABLESPOON GRATED ORANGE ZEST

2 EGGS

½ TEASPOON VANILLA EXTRACT

¼ TEASPOON ALMOND EXTRACT

1½ CUPS COARSELY CHOPPED
ALMONDS

Preheat oven to 325° F.

In a medium bowl, combine flour, anise seeds, baking powder and salt; set aside. Beat butter, sugar and orange zest, using an electric mixer until light and fluffy. Beat in eggs, one at a time; add vanilla and almond extracts. Gradually beat in flour mixture. Stir in almonds. Divide dough in half. On an ungreased baking sheet, form into two flattened logs, each one about 14 inches long by 3 inches wide. Place 3 inches apart on baking sheet. Bake 40 minutes or until light golden color. Reduce oven temperature to 250° F. On a cutting board, cut logs crosswise on the diagonal into ¾-inch slices. Arrange biscotti cut-side down on baking sheet. Bake 10 minutes on each side. Transfer biscotti onto a rack to cool. Store in an airtight container.

Makes about 3 dozen.

Five Brothers Culinary Club

Share the Passion!
Join the Five Brothers Culinary Club

Send us your name and address on a 3 I/2 x 5 card
and you will periodically receive our free newsletter
filled with inventive recipes and creative food ideas
for unforgettable home meals.

Mail to: FIVE BROTHERS CULINARY CLUB
P.O. BOX 1210-B
GRAND RAPIDS, MN 55745-1210